Online Learning

What You Need to Know to Succeed

Kevin C. Kays, Ph.D., N.C.C.

Copyright © 2019 by Kevin Kays

Sentia Publishing Company has the exclusive rights to reproduce this work, to prepare derivative works from this work, to publicly distribute this work, to publicly perform this work, and to publicly display this work.

All rights reserved. No part of this publication may be reproduced, stored in a retrieval system, or transmitted, in any form or by any means, electronic, mechanical, photocopying, recording, or otherwise, without the prior written permission of the copyright owner.

Printed in the United States of America
ISBN 978-1-7337412-3-1

Table of Contents

Introduction v

Section 1: Why Online? 1

Section 2: Selecting a Program That Is Right for You 4

Section 3: Equipment, Software and Textbooks That You Need to Get Started 8

Section 4: Support (Friends, Family, and Coworkers): Keeping It Going 10

Section 5: Time Management 14

Section 6: What Kind of a Learner Are You? 18

Section 7: Motivation 21

Section 8: Quick Start and How to Get into a Routine 26

Section 9: Starting with the End in Mind: Goal Setting 28

Section 10: Hitting the "Brick Wall" within the Course 30

Section 11: Utilize Your Resources: Working Smarter 32

Section 12: Personalizing the Online Experience: Connecting with Faculty 34

Section 13: Keep Moving, Eat Right, and Sleep 36

Section 14: Test Taking 39

Section 15: Celebrating Your Significant Accomplishment: Finishing the Chapter! 43

Conclusion 46

Introduction

Taking online courses can be intimidating for anyone who is new to the experience. Even if you have taken online courses in the past, there are tips that can make you more successful. This book will provide best practices for how to succeed in and get the most out of the courses you take online, including how to identify the right online program for you and determining the proper equipment for each course. The material in this book can be personalized to your experience—take what works for you and add to it. You can excel at your online courses. This book will help you to get there.

Section 1
Why Online?

Why should you take a class online, or even complete your entire degree program online? Is this really what's right for you? It all depends on you and what your needs are. There are numerous advantages to taking a course online or getting a degree online. The initial attraction may be the same thing that attracts people to online shopping: It's convenient and can save a lot of time driving, finding a place to park, and paying for parking and gas. You can avoid going out in bad weather, fighting through crowds of people, and any possible viruses that might be lurking about.

For many people, online learning can be as good as, and often even better than, traditional classroom learning. Online learning offers more flexibility. You can choose what works best for your learning experience. You can listen to lectures in the privacy of your bedroom, in your office at work, at a restaurant, or even while going for a jog. Online learning allows you to fit your course or courses around your work schedule more easily. Some courses don't even have a set meeting time, which gives you even more flexibility.

We all know the "power-at-our-fingertips" feeling that the internet can bring to so many things that come up in our daily lives. With online courses, both the power and the learning are also at our fingertips. But you might feel that you'd be missing out on interactions with people by taking an online course. Many online courses have chat rooms set up for students and instructors. There may even be pages on social networks that are devoted to these courses. You can chat online with others literally 24 hours a day! But what if that's not enough and you want verbal or even face-to-face interactions with classmates and teachers or instructors?

You might be surprised to know that many online courses offer verbal and even face-to-face interactions with students in cohorts that are taking your class and instructors who are teaching these courses. They even offer one-on-one interactions with instructors using video chat if you would like. Screen sharing, where the person working with you can see what you are looking at on your screen, or you can see theirs, is also common so instructors can help you with your work and guide you through problems.

But what if you need a tutor? Can you get a tutor online? You may be thinking of the tutors in the past that you had to sit down with face-to-face to go over your questions. There are tutors available online as well that are willing and able to help. The wonderful thing about online courses is that you can be interacting with other students and renowned teachers from all around the world, and you don't even need to leave the house.

Online learning can teach you to be more self-disciplined and therefore more successful. With an online course, you will not have someone standing in front of you, staring you down with a list of deadlines. You will have to spend time on your own getting organized, managing your time, and motivating yourself to get the work done that is required for the course.

This is a wonderful skill that looks great to bosses or future employers who know what it takes to be successful online.

Online learning can help you get that job you have always wanted or advance in your current job. Before, the course you wanted to take or the degree you wanted to obtain was unattainable due to the location of the institution or time required to drive to and be in class. But now you can pursue your dreams. If you have a computer, internet, and electricity, you have endless possibilities for your education. The world is so much smaller today, and this is a tremendous advantage to anyone who takes advantage of it.

These are only a handful of examples of the benefits of online learning—there are many, many more out there. Are online courses as good as face-to-face courses? Depending on the course, they can be even better. It is up to you to decide which is the best fit for you.

Section 2
Selecting a Program That Is Right for You

You've made up your mind that you need a degree and decided that getting your degree online makes the most sense for you. Remember, this degree is for you and should be the best fit for you. There are a lot of different programs out there, and everyone has their own opinion depending on their own experiences or what they've heard, but you need to do what makes the most sense for you. With that in mind, consider the following:

What program is the best fit?
A lot of factors will play into selecting an online program. One thing to consider is the curriculum. Do they offer the degree that is best suited for your needs? What is their delivery

method? Can you make the meetings with the teacher or professor, the class "groups," tutoring sessions, etc.?

What is the primary age group this program is designed to serve? Is it the K-through-12 student, traditional-aged college student, or the nontraditional-aged college student? Is this for the full-time student or the part-time student? Does the student population work and have families? These are all important questions since there will be different expectations for the different groups.

Passion

Do you have a passion for this program? Does the curriculum inspire you? There will always be courses to take that are not inspiring, but does the core curriculum "fit" with you and the direction you want to go with your career?

If the passion and drive are not there, you may waste a lot of time and money on this degree program. You may decide to drop out because of this, or, if you obtain your degree, you may be unhappy with the career you just spent so much time and money on. Be wise, be smart, and find the right fit for you.

Reviews

It is always a good idea to see what others have to say about the program. Sure, there are always going to be reviews from people who had a bad experience, and reviews that make the program sound too good to be true, but average these out and there should be enough quality reviews that you can get a good idea if this is a solid, student-centered program that is right for you.

Sometimes you pick up some things in reviews that you didn't even think about. If you are still interested in this program, write down these concerns and share them with the admissions office or enrollment representative. See if they can shed any light on the subject, answer your questions, and dispel your concerns.

Support and How Interactive Is This Program

Is the program that you are interested in one that has help for students? And how interactive is it? If you have a question or concern, will you be directed to a written answer copied out of a manual or a real live person? How accessible is the help you need? You may not think of this when starting a program, but problems do arise, and questions need to be answered.

You should be looking for a program that answers questions quickly and effectively. There should be a real person to help with the concerns you have and to follow up later to make sure that you are still doing well. Slow response time, incomplete answers, or answers that don't make sense should raise multiple red flags.

Cost and Financial Assistance

How much is tuition? Are there any additional administrative fees? How long will it take to get your degree and what will be the final cost? Does this program have any financial assistance that can help defer the price tag?

You don't want to start a degree program to find out down the road that you can't finish because you can't afford the total price, or your financial assistance will not cover the cost of the entire degree. What are the other costs you may be expected to cover? It's not a good sign when there are hidden costs you only discover once you have officially enrolled. All costs should be explained up front so there are no surprises.

You should also check into what type of financial assistance there may be to help you defer the costs of your degree program. Make sure to inquire about scholarships, grants, loans, and other types of aid. Find out if the institution has money available to offset the cost, especially money that will not have to be paid back.

Once you get this degree, will it pay for itself? What is the average income of a graduate of this program? Will you be eligible for a raise or promotion after you get your degree? These are all important points to consider.

Is Travel Involved?

Does this online program require any travel to meet the requirements of the program? Will you need to travel for exam proctoring? Will you need to meet face-to-face with advisors or complete a residency on-site? Can you satisfy these requirements?

These requirements should be explained up front, but sometimes they are hidden deep in some online paperwork. If you can't find the answers yourself, make sure to ask the admissions officer or enrollment representative and use the information to help you make an educated decision about the program.

Accreditation

Will the program that you are interested in do what you think it will do once you graduate? Will it get you into that undergraduate or graduate program or qualify you for the job you want? For most online programs, a regional accreditation for university academics and a national accreditation for online programs are the basic standard that most people look for in a program.

Do some research to find out the accrediting bodies for your program and ask the enrollment representative about this as well. Compare programs to see which ones have the backing and credentials that are expected for your institution and degree. This can affect not only your chances at future jobs or other educational institutions but also with receiving loans or aid that you are depending on to help you complete this program. Accreditation makes a difference when you try to use your degree after you earn it.

Section 3
Equipment, Software, and Textbooks That You Need to Get Started

One important area to explore and prepare for when getting ready to start an online program is the equipment. What software and textbooks you will need? Most programs will tell you up front what is needed, but you may need to ask if not.

Also explore what equipment can and cannot be used. For instance, most programs will tell you that a laptop or desktop computer and an internet connection are all you need, but does the program also use other electronic devices, such as tablets or smartphones? Do you need special software? Is this sold separately or provided free of charge? Is a specific web browser required?

Another thing to consider when thinking about equipment is not just what you can get by with but also what equipment will help you really succeed as a student. If you have the space, consider setting up dual screens at your computer. This will allow you to have multiple windows open at once, which will save you the time and headache of flipping back and forth. A cordless mouse is a simple add-on, but it can also make life a little easier. If your course involves a lot of audio or talking, a nice headset with earphones and a mic will also be beneficial.

Does the program require you to purchase expensive textbooks? Some programs offer access to online textbooks that are included in the tuition, whereas other programs require you to purchase these items on your own. If this is the case, it can be a significant out-of-pocket expense that you did not budget for. The cost of one textbook can be a significant amount. Is the online version available for purchase or will you need to buy the printed version? Can you buy a used copy, or do they require the most recent edition? Is the book available at your local library? Will the book you are using help in future courses or in your professional career?

Once you purchase these books you may not be able to use them again. You may be able to resell them, but usually only at a fraction of the price you paid for them. If you need the book for future courses or for reference material for your career, buying the book could be a good investment, but no matter the answer, you need to factor in the cost for your program.

Be sure to check all the potential "extra" expenses up front to determine cost, and make sure you have everything you need from day one. You don't want to start a semester two weeks behind because you weren't ready.

Section 4
Support (Friends, Family, and Coworkers): Keeping It Going

It is important for you to have support while completing an online degree. Some of you might be thinking you are an island and you don't need anyone's help. This can be true for some, but most everyone else should have a solid support network who can be there for you on good days and not-so-good days alike.

   A support system is not to be confused with the several hundred "likes" one might get on social media when you announce you are going back to school, or just passed a test. That may be enough for some, but what you really need are people who will be there for you, support you, and help you to keep going throughout the program whether you ask them to or not. They know the degree is important to you and they will ask how you are doing, cheer you on, and lift you up—not just at the beginning, but throughout. Establishing a solid support structure is important for the success of the student.

Part of this burden lies on you, the student, though. You may be thinking, "How is this my responsibility? I am the one that should be supported, and want to be supported, by others." Communication is the key. Some of your supporters may ask you every day how you are doing. But ultimately, whether asked or not, you must communicate to them what is going on. How can someone wish you luck on a test unless they know you are taking one? How can they know you just did poorly on a paper unless you let them know? Communication is key to having good, solid support.

The support issue can go in the opposite direction if you are not careful as well. Where there once was support when you started the program, after a while, the newness and excitement wear off and it's back to the day-to-day grind. If there is no communication, then both parties may build a certain amount of resentment. You, the student, may feel like you are not getting supported enough. This may be through verbal support or taking care of other important matters like children or daily chores.

The other person may be building resentment as well. They may be starting to resent the classes that are drawing you away from the family or them. The way to combat this is communication and understanding. It is very, very important to have this when you start the program, but it is even more important that the topic is revisited often throughout. Maybe it's simply a reminder how important this degree is to your future as a couple or as a family. Maybe it's a reminder that this is a means to an end—it will not go on forever, just until the degree is obtained. But both sides need to be open and honest with their feelings on how this is affecting them.

Once you've talked this out, you can look for solutions to help deal with these feelings without giving up on the goal of your degree. No one said that obtaining a university degree would be easy. It can be challenging on several fronts, but if you work through the problems and concerns and keep moving forward daily toward your goal of graduation, it will come.

Here are a few ideas that can help with support and communication.

- *In addition to talking about what is going on, you can use a family calendar to post important dates, like when a test will occur, or a paper is due.* You can even post your study schedule, so everyone knows this is your time to study.

- *Another idea is to ask for help.* If you have too much going on and feel like you are sinking, ask others to help you before it goes from bad to worse. Maybe this is babysitting the children so you can take a test, study, or write a paper. It could be asking someone to walk the dog for you.

    Most people are happy to help, especially if they know they are helping you to achieve such an important goal. But don't expect them to ask you; you should ask them. Also, don't forget to thank them once they have helped. If you don't thank the person who helped you, they may feel like you didn't appreciate their help and may be less inclined to help in the future. A simple thank-you can go a long way.

- *Something else that can help with support is to use the carrot method.* Place a reward for you and your significant other and/or family once you successfully reach a goal. It could be going out for a nice dinner once you submit that huge paper or getting away for a weekend once you passed the test. You need to take some time to celebrate, and it is important to recognize your supporters as well.

- *You can also just do something simple, like buy some flowers or candy to say thank you for their continued support.* Maybe a simple thank-you note. You know what the other person likes, and a small gesture can be worth a thousand thank-you's.

You may be thinking you are too busy for any of this. Is it even worth it? Sure, it sounds nice, but you're too busy to do any of this, right? Wrong! If you fail to communicate and don't foster a feeling of teamwork and support, then everything will start to unravel very quickly. You may find that the burden is too great to continue.

The key is to start early communication about your degree program and what is needed, and to communicate often. Never take for granted the support that is being given to you, and always be thankful when you receive it. The reality is, getting a degree is a team effort. Support each other and you will ultimately win, but if you don't, you will lose.

Section 5
Time Management

You may think you are good with time—that is, until you add too many things to your plate. Unless you are someone who has nothing but free time on your hands, adding an online degree can be a major change to your schedule. For an already busy and packed schedule, adding hours of class and study time means something else on your schedule must give—not necessarily forever, but at least until you accomplish your degree.

It is important to keep the necessities on your new schedule. Don't forget to budget time for eating and sleeping! And if you are working, that will take up a large chunk of your time as well. But there can be other things that have to be part of this new schedule. You should plan out a daily schedule and include time to study. Most online programs that are for full-time students will ask for you to plan out a minimum of 20 hours a week to study. This is doable but, as mentioned, something typically must give.

To be successful with an online program, your study routine must become habit. Many people start a program with excitement and enthusiasm, but after the first few weeks the excitement goes away. Students start to look for time on the weekends or next week when studying will be more convenient. But if you don't plan it out and make time for studying or schoolwork, you won't do it until the night before you have an exam, or a major paper is due. It will be too little, too late, and you are doomed to fail--or at the very least not perform as well as you could. Keeping a consistent study schedule will not only make you a successful student but will also save you a lot of stress and anxiety.

Here are some techniques that may help you keep the studying going.

Squeezing in Some Schoolwork:
A 15-Minute Technique to Help Procrastination

The 15-minute rule can be a great tool for getting you started. Pick a task to do for 15 minutes, no matter how big or small it may be. It doesn't matter if you face distractions or you are not in a mood to do it; whatever the reason, just do it for 15 minutes.

After the 15 minutes are up, you can to stop working if you feel like it. You can, however, decide to continue working. Many people find that once they start a task and keep it going for a few minutes, they are more than likely to continue until the task is finished, even if they didn't feel like doing it to begin with.

This technique works best when you set a regular, reoccurring time each day to study. By doing this, you will be setting up a habit, or routine that will pay big dividends with your study time. You should not be *looking* for time to study. If you look for the time, you will never find it. If you *make* the time, even small steps to begin with, it will happen.

Utilize the "Wasted" Time on Your Schedule

Everyone has "wasted" time on their schedules—times they are waiting for a friend to meet you, or for that next meeting to start, or for the bus or train to arrive, when there is nothing to do but wait. You can make good use of this time, whether it's just a couple of minutes or much longer. Many online programs have an app you can log in to using your phone or tablet to go over material. You can even print off material or make up your own flashcards for this purpose.

You might be wondering, "How is only a few minutes going to help me learn this material?" Many studies on the subject have found that studying more often for shorter intervals is more beneficial than a marathon study session. The repetitive act of going over this material can help the brain retain the information. You can even do this while eating breakfast, lunch, or dinner. Rather than playing a game on your phone or reading the news or checking the score from last night's game, you can use this time for something that can really make a difference for an upcoming test.

Chunking Work to Avoid Procrastinating

Many times, we put off work because it is difficult for us. An important step you can take to help overcome procrastination is to break down a task into smaller and smaller chunks. Keep breaking down a task into smaller tasks until you feel comfortable doing that mini-task.

For example, if you are required to write a lengthy report for an assignment, or read a long article, it often becomes difficult to motivate yourself to sit down and make yourself work. This often results in endless procrastination.

However, try to break it down to smaller and smaller parts. Instead of trying to write the entire report or read the article all at once, try to write just a couple of paragraphs or read just a couple of pages. Once you complete those couple of paragraphs or read those couple of pages, you might find it much easier to continue for a larger chunk, or even until you finish.

Often when you start out with the intention of writing a complete paper or reading an entire article, especially at the end of a workday, you simply can't find the energy or motivation. If you don't feel that you can complete the entire assignment and want to quit after reading or writing only a few sentences, you still will have accomplished something. Maybe the assignment can be finished in the next day or two.

Another technique that is effective when writing a paper is to start by putting together an outline. Use the instructor's directions to write down the important items that are needed in the paper. Then use these important items to put together an outline. These are the main points that you want to get across throughout the body of your paper. At this point, research the important points in your outline. Then, go back and start to fill in the outline with the content from your research. Once you have the body of the paper written, you can write your introduction paragraph and conclusion, basing these on the content of your paper. This is a technique that helps you to break down the paper into smaller chunks and makes it easier to write.

Section 6
What Kind of a Learner Are You?

It is important to discover what your learning style is and how you can utilize this for your new program. Some online programs will have different types of learning resources that can fit the needs of a wide range of students. Utilize the material that best fits your learning style, and if you don't see it offered, ask for it. Also, don't be afraid to try out new learning resources. Regardless of the type of learner you are, diversifying your learning by using different methods can keep the material fresh and interesting.

Below are a few tips that may help you:

> ➢ *Focus on learning in more than one way.* You may like to listen to a podcast, which involves auditory learning, or learning by listening. You may want to consider rehearsing or going over the information that you need

to learn, both verbally and visually. This could involve describing this information to a friend or taking notes. By learning in multiple ways, you're further increasing your knowledge base. When you do this, you are more likely to be learning the material as opposed to just memorizing it. This will make it much easier when it comes test time.

➢ *It is well-known in the teaching community that a great way to learn material is to teach it to someone else.* If you can explain it to someone else, it will help you get a firm grasp on the material yourself. Therefore, some teachers require students to do class presentations. It's not solely to help students with their public speaking skills or to get over the nervousness of standing in front of the class, but also of knowing that if the student can know the material well enough to present on it, or teach it, to the rest of the class, they are solidifying that information in their own minds.

You can do this same thing. Try to put the information in your own words. Teach it to someone else. You can use your new information on a friend or family member, or you can use this during a group discussion with other classmates. You can also explain it to the teacher or instructor to make sure you fully understand the material.

➢ *Another great technique when learning new information is to connect the material you are learning to material you already know.* If you can connect the material from the course to an experience from real life, you are much more likely to fully understand it and the material is much more likely to stay in your memory because it is connected to other memories rather than being isolated.

You can also solidify the information you just learned by putting this into practice. Take the material out of the classroom and use it in your life. For instance, if you are taking a course about a foreign language, when you come out of the classroom, use this language. If you are taking a course about how to manage people or work with people, take this information to work with you and try it out. The more you use it, the more it will make sense, and it will stick in your memory longer.

➤ *If you don't know the answer, look it up.* Research has shown that if you are struggling to remember information or you don't know the answer, you should simply look it up instead of continuing to try and remember. Why is that? It's because the continued struggle causes your brain to create an error state, and that is what you "remember" the next time you get the same question.

Looking up the answer, even if you must do it multiple times, will trigger the brain to come up with the correct answer—kind of like using a flashcard. You see the question on one side, and if you don't know the answer, or even if you do, your brain immediately sees the correct answer when you flip the card over and stores it for the future. It is a useful technique that really works.

Section 7
Motivation

What Is Your Ultimate Goal?

What motivates you to get your degree? Why are you doing this? You should write out all the reasons why you are getting this degree. Are you doing this to get a job? To get a better job? To make more money perhaps? Is it a promise you made to yourself, or maybe a promise you made to someone else? Is there a legacy you want to leave behind?

There are a lot of possible reasons, and most people have more than one. Write these down and keep these somewhere safe so you can always find it. You should then type out your answers and print them off on a single piece of paper. Put this piece of paper up someplace you will see it. This can serve as a great way to keep you motivated even in tough times or just as a daily reminder of why you are doing this.

Down the road, when the coursework gets tough, when maybe there are outside factors in your life that are pulling you away from your courses and your goal, look at this piece of paper. Read all the reasons why you are doing this. This is a wonderful motivator to help you to keep moving forward toward graduation. It is important to keep your fire burning. The basic question is, what drives you? The answer is not only why you are here but why you will also succeed.

Reward Yourself When You Accomplish a Goal

You may have already heard of this, or even done it in the past. The point with this approach is to set up a task or goal to complete and then make up a reward for yourself if you complete this task. This can be used for large and small goals. It can be for passing a class or just reading a chapter.

The reward can be whatever you want it to be. You can reward yourself with a bowl of ice cream for reading the next chapter or going to the movies when you get that "A" you worked so hard for. You can even tell yourself that as soon as you finish the paper you are writing, you will go for a walk with the dog—that's a reward for you and the dog. Also, as we already covered, you can even make it a family reward. The reward for the entire family could be going out for dinner, going to the fun house, or going to the cinema.

The idea, of course, is to have a reward attached to your goal as incentive and motivation. This will also help you complete future tasks or goals, because you know that there are smaller rewards leading up to the reason why you are doing all of this: to graduate!

Persistence and Positive Attitude

What does a positive attitude have to do with anything, you ask? Everything! Henry Ford once said, "Whether you think you can, or you think you can't, you're right!" I believe that is true. If you tell yourself you won't make it to graduation, or tell yourself you can't pass a course, I believe you will absolutely fail. But if you stick with it and tell yourself repeatedly that you will pass, you will graduate; and if you put this into action, I firmly believe you will succeed. The power of positive thinking is no joke. It really does have an impact, and it can make or break your online experience.

Persistence is also a vital behavior to being successful with your degree and everything else you pursue in life. As a student, you will run into numerous roadblocks; you will be knocked down multiple times; at times you will struggle and even wonder if you can really do this. Some people call it grit; others call it persistence. What you must do when you run into tough times is to bear down and keep moving forward. Sink your teeth into this class or degree and don't give up. The easiest thing in the world to do is to quit. That takes no effort at all, and there are all kinds of excuses that can be made to justify it. But to persist and accomplish your goal…that is the mark of a true winner.

The bottom line is, how important is this degree to you? If it is truly important to you, it will also be something that you will make happen come good times or bad. *Persistence* and a *positive attitude* can help you accomplish your goals and make your dreams come true. Write these two words down—put them on your refrigerator or someplace you will see them daily to remind yourself that you WILL succeed, and your persistence and positive attitude will be instrumental in getting you there.

Take a Break

It is also good to take a break from time to time so you don't burn out. Take a day or a weekend off. You need the break to recharge your mental batteries. But it's also important that after you take this break, you get back into your study routine right away. It's okay to step away if you know that you must return to finish what you set out to do.

Sometimes a break can help you refocus your efforts or even see things in a new light once you return. You don't want to get to the point of burnout. You are the best person to know when you need a break and when you can keep pushing forward. Just keep in mind your goal for the day, the week, the month, the semester, and your ultimate goal of earning your degree.

Support

Your online program should have professionals who are ready and willing to help you. They should have academic support, learning success support, disability support, and support for veterans, among other areas.

What kind of support do you have at home? Who is encouraging you when you feel like putting work off or giving up? Who is helping foster an environment for success while you study? Who is helping you focus on graduation? Surround yourself with support! There are LOTS of people ready and willing to cheer you on! Remember—this is temporary. Soon, the degree will be yours, and you'll be so glad you pushed through and made this DREAM your REALITY!

So, remember—your success isn't automatic. It won't happen overnight. It's the grit and determination that will get you through to the end, to finally realize your goal and dream of graduation.

Section 8
Quick Start and How to Get into a Routine

Successes build positive energy, and they also build a confidence to keep moving forward. Little successes can lead to bigger ones. Each success is a building block that can be used for bigger and better things to come. If you can start your program, or term, with a quick win, that will give you momentum to build upon that success with the next course(s). Even within the course itself, start with the easier material and build upon that success before you jump into the challenging stuff. Starting with success early is what many refer to as a "quick start". Hitting it hard early and building upon this success is a key to your overall success for the course and the degree.

The second part of that is getting into a routine. It is important to make the time for studying and to not be searching for the time. The most successful students are those that sit down with a schedule that shows the week by day and the day by hour and plot out when they will be studying. They mark it off and then they stick to this routine. This time is treated with respect and is ONLY for studying.

I had a student who told me he treats this scheduled time with his coursework like a second job. He told me that he is always on time and he gives 100% all the time, devoted only to coursework. If someone calls, he lets it go to voicemail; if he receives a text, he waits until study time is over to text them back; and if a friend asks him to have coffee, he picks a time that is outside of study time, just like he does when he is working.

The routine is what will bring you success. If you are someone who says, "This weekend, I should have time," or "Next week will be better," you are setting yourself up for failure. If you are looking for the time, you will never find it or never find nearly enough to be successful as an online student. If this degree is important, just like anything else in your life, you will make time for it. If it's not important, you won't, and then it won't be there, or you will fail.

Think about treating your study schedule like going to work. If you only go to work when you want to go to work, then you won't have a job for very long. Or think about it like a relationship: If you don't make time for a relationship then it probably won't be there for long. An online degree is much the same: you make time for it, treat it like a second job, and your success rate will skyrocket. If you don't, you will likely fail out and you will be looking for excuses why you started but never graduated.

Don't be that person that is making up excuses; be that person who has the degree in hand. Excuses aren't worth anything—a degree is.

Section 9
Starting with the End in Mind: Goal Setting

Goal setting is very important for success for any student, whether online or otherwise. You should have a goal to graduate, and you should have a goal for what you will do with your degree beyond graduation. But you should also have a goal for each individual course. If you start with the end in mind, you are much more likely to realize the success of reaching your goal.

Visualizing your goals is important but so is making a plan of action. Break it down. When's your first test date? When is your first paper due? Look at the syllabus and the calendar and work backward from there. On what dates will you complete certain sections or take practice quizzes? If you need to write a paper, when will you have certain sections complete? Give yourself deadlines.

The big goals should be broken down into smaller, more manageable goals and by completing the small goals you will accomplish the big goals. As the saying goes, "Rome wasn't built in a day," and neither is a degree. If you plan things out on a calendar, work to hit your smaller goals, then your big goal will be easily accomplished.

Section 10
Hitting the "Brick Wall" within the Course

One common problem that many students encounter is "stalling out." You are working at a good pace, accomplishing your goals, and staying persistent and positive—and then something happens, and you hit a wall. This figurative wall is not something that should be taken lightly. Some walls have caused students to completely give up. But the good news is the wall can be overcome.

The first step is to recognize that you have stalled out and are not going anywhere. The second step is to act. Oftentimes you must take action that you have not taken before in other courses. You can't just approach this course the same way you have always approached your courses in the past. Try something new. Look for advice from someone else who has experience with this course—the instructor, professor, or a mentor may be good people to talk to.

For most problems, you have two choices (not including giving up, because that is NOT a choice we will take). You can either power through it or go around your problem and then come back to it. Both can work, and it is up to you as to which way is the best. *Powering through* is taking that bulldog mentality, gritting your teeth, and giving it everything you have. *Going around it* is planning to keep working and keep moving ahead, with the goal of coming back to the problem that is stopping you. It's also about not losing time and to keep moving forward.

Once you have your confidence and momentum built back up, you can look at the problem again with a new perspective and a new attitude. The main thing is to not let the wall you are facing get the best of you. Do you want this degree or not? If the answer is yes, you WILL make it happen.

Section 11
Utilize Your Resources: Working Smarter

Each course you will encounter will have a lot of information. I mean *a lot*! There has been a lot researched and written about almost every subject out there. You will encounter an ocean's worth of material—and if you don't work smart, you will end up adrift in the middle of this ocean not knowing what's important or which way to go.

It is important to not only work hard but to work smart. Most instructors or professors will provide learning resources to help identify the most important areas to focus on. Most textbooks will even point to the important points to be learned. If you don't know what's important, ask. Utilizing the learning resources that you have is like taking that ocean's worth of water and having it handed to you in more drinkable glassfuls.

Be cautious when using outside sources, as tempting as they may be. Almost anything can be found on the internet, that doesn't mean it's true. It might look good but, in the end, you may realize you just wasted a lot of time and energy going down a rabbit hole only to discover that to find out that the information you found was useless.

You can always talk to your instructor, professor, or mentor and ask them about resources you have found, and, if they endorse them, you can proceed; otherwise, don't waste your time. Work hard but also work smart.

---

*"It's not that I'm so smart, it's just that
I stay with problems longer."
Albert Einstein*

Section 12
Personalizing the Online Experience: Connecting with Faculty

It is common knowledge that students who connect with course instructors are the ones most likely to not only pass the course but also graduate from the institution. But you may be thinking, *this is online! I won't see the faculty; how will I connect with them?*

The most successful students will make a point to talk to the course instructor for the course early, and they will also talk with them often. This has so many benefits. For one, course instructors have the inside track on what it will take to pass this course, and by talking to them regularly, you will learn this as well. It will save you time and a lot of headaches by following their advice. And, who doesn't want to save time, and headache, to pass a course?

But the secondary benefit is also very real. Once you get to know and connect with the faculty, you have a connection with the university—someone who you can go to for advice even after the course is over, even someone who can potentially help you beyond graduation. You don't have to go it alone; the faculty is there to help you. You just need to take advantage of them and what they have to offer.

Section 13
Keep Moving, Eat Right, and Sleep

Your first thought when thinking about "keep moving" may be to keep moving forward regardless of any obstacles you may run into. But didn't we already cover this? Persistence, right? While persistence and a positive attitude are extremely important to being successful for this degree, and anything else you may decide to pursue, this section is not addressing that. I'm talking about literally keeping your body moving.

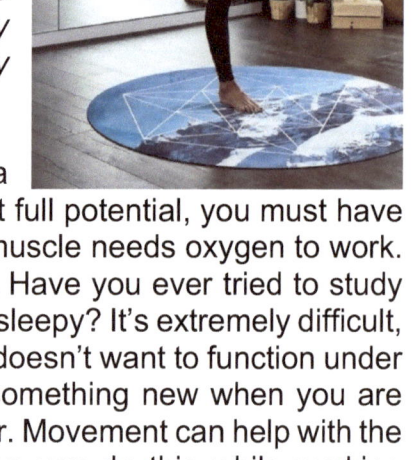

Now you may be thinking, *how do I do this? I'm on the computer, it's online—the only things that are moving are my fingers.*

Okay, let me explain.

Think about the brain as a muscle. For a muscle to work at full potential, you must have proper blood flowing to it. The muscle needs oxygen to work. The brain has the same needs. Have you ever tried to study when getting very tired, or even sleepy? It's extremely difficult, to say the least. Your brain just doesn't want to function under those conditions. Try to learn something new when you are alert and awake; it's much easier. Movement can help with the brain staying alert. But how can you do this while working online? There are a lot of ways:

- *Take planned breaks to do some quick exercises.* These may simply be a few stretches or yoga positions. Something to get the blood flowing through your body again. You can even walk around, do some push-ups or sit-ups, or whatever exercise you feel like your body can do quickly to get the blood flowing again.
- *Try studying while walking on a treadmill.* This may be a little challenging for some, but it keeps the blood flowing, which energizes the body.
- *Try studying standing up.* There are so many health benefits to standing versus sitting. Among others, it helps to improve your energy and improve your mood.
- *You can even do stretches and exercises while sitting in your chair. This also has numerous benefits by providing oxygen to your muscles. Better blood flow helps your energy level and your general wellness.*

These are just a few ideas to keep your brain working at peak efficiency. What you want to avoid is getting into that comfortable recliner, or propped up by pillows in bed, and reading until you fall asleep. Your body will associate this place with "shutting down" and sleep, and it will become a losing battle.

You should also avoid using sugar or caffeine to help you to stay alert. A coffee or soda, or even snacking every now and then, may not be immediately harmful, but overuse can cause health risks that can have long-term effects. A little planned movement can be much better than snacking for your brain. When your brain is too tired to study, take a break.

Sleep is also important for your brain. It is important to get the recommended daily amount of sleep. If you don't have enough sleep, you won't be able to concentrate, and your brain will not retain the information it needs. As with your study schedule, your sleep schedule should be planned and regular. It is critical to have enough sleep for your brain to operate at its peak efficiency.

You should consult your physician or health-care professional regarding the best approach for you for diet and exercise. Everyone's body has different needs and restrictions, but the important thing is that eating healthy and keeping your body active will also improve how your brain functions, which can have a direct, positive impact on your courses.

Section 14
Test Taking

You have studied and prepared the best that you can for your upcoming test. Keep in mind, your best performance on an exam is directly related to the preparation that you put into the exam. If you have studied and taken full advantage of the available learning resources, you should be ready to take and pass the test.

Here are a few things to keep in mind before you take an exam:

- *Get plenty of rest the night before.* Lack of sleep can severely impair how you answer a question. Review the material the night before and then get a good night's sleep. You will think much clearer by doing this.

- *Eat energy- or protein-rich food the day of the test.* Consider eating eggs, nuts, yogurt, and fresh fruit. You don't want to eat too much right before the final. A full stomach may cause you to feel tired while your body is digesting all that food. You also don't want to go hungry and not eat anything. Your brain needs energy to keep functioning at full potential.

- *Have a glass or bottle of water to sip throughout the exam (unless the exam is in-person and drinks are not allowed).* Before the test, a protein-rich drink can also help.

- *Before beginning the exam, review the material.* Skim through and focus on the highlighted areas. This will refresh your mind and you may even catch something that will stick in your short-term memory that you didn't already have memorized.

- *Get set up early.* Find out where you need to be if it is a proctored site or be sure to get logged into the testing site early if you are taking the test from home.

  If going to a proctored site, check it out the day before taking. Find out where the proctoring center is located, where to park, and what is expected of you when you get there. Whether taking the test at a proctoring center or online, ask what proper identification is needed and what you can have during the test.

  If taking the test online make sure you have the correct website and you have downloaded the correct program if needed. Make sure your internet speed is fast enough and you have the correct web camera if needed. You should do all of this in advance and not wait until the test is about to begin. By doing this, you can concentrate on the test and not worry about being surprised at the last minute.

What to Do When Taking the Online Test

- Make sure you know how many questions you must answer, what types of questions there will be, how much each type of question is worth, and how much time you have to complete the test. To be a successful test taker, you should plan out your time and pace yourself throughout the test.

  You don't want to spend most of your time on multiple choice questions that are only worth a small percentage of the grade when the essay questions, which are worth most of the test, are left undone because they are at the end and you didn't have time to finish them.

- While taking an online test, check to see if you can come back to questions that you answered at the beginning of the test later in the test. If you get stuck on a question, skip it and come back to it if you can. If you can't go back, take your best educated guess.

Don't waste time or let your confidence slip away just because there were a few tough questions early in the test. Some test writers will intentionally put the toughest questions early to blow your confidence or, at the very minimum, make you lose a lot of time on those questions so you will have to rush through the remainder. You don't want to fall into this trap. It's possible a future question can even help you answer an earlier question or trigger a memory that will help you.

➢ Follow the basics of taking a test:
   A. *Read the question and all the answers (if it's multiple choice) thoroughly, even repeatedly.* Make sure you know what the question is asking and what the answers are telling you.
   B. *Eliminate the answers you know are not correct.* This process of elimination could help you to ignore all but one answer, which could be the correct one.
   C. *Go with your gut.* Sometimes you may not be sure, but you have a strong feeling; your "gut" tells you it's a certain answer. Go with that. Unless you find definite evidence later that you chose incorrectly, don't go back and change your answer.

➢ *Pace yourself.* You do not want to go too slow and run out of time on the test, but you don't want to go too fast, either. When you go too fast, you may miss important information that will help you answer the questions.

I once heard a wise teacher ask her class, "What does the person who finishes this test first get?" The class thought there was a wonderful prize to get to the finish line first. After several guesses of wonderful prizes, the teacher told her class the answer. She said, "The first person who finishes this test will get an 'F.'" The class was shocked and confused.

The teacher explained, "I'm not going to give you an 'F' because you are the first one done, but by being the first one done, in most cases, you have hurried the test and missed many questions simply because you were not thorough enough. You will earn the 'F' by being careless and not answering the test questions correctly."

Being first doesn't always mean you are going to fail; there must be someone who completes the test before others in the class. But the point was not lost on the class, and they never forgot this story. Take the time you need and be thorough. Watch the clock and your place in the test. Pace yourself all the way through.

- *If you run into any problems during the test, let the proctor know immediately.* They may not be able to see you are having trouble with the internet connection or the program is malfunctioning. Do not assume everyone can see what you can see.

- *Confidence!* Stay confident throughout the test. Remember, with most tests, you don't have to answer every question correctly. You can miss some questions and still pass the test. Keep reminding yourself that you prepared thoroughly, and you will have a much better chance to pass.

- *At the conclusion of the test, make sure your test has been successfully submitted and the proctor has everything they need from you before you log off.*

Section 15
Celebrating Your Significant Accomplishment: Finishing the Chapter!

Do you celebrate when you pass that test or that paper? You should. It is important to reward yourself for these accomplishments. A proven success technique is to even plan out a reward for when you do pass that test or paper.

Do you also celebrate when you pass the course? You should. Each step closer to graduation should be celebrated. You have accomplished the significant goal that you set for yourself and you deserve to do something nice for yourself. This can inspire you to keep moving forward. Even if that celebration is just a short break from courses, it is something to look forward to and even motivate you to accomplish your next goal.

Once you finish your degree, will you attend graduation or commencement? Maybe the better question is, why *wouldn't* you attend? You worked tremendously hard to do what some say couldn't be done. You accomplished your goal with hours, days, weeks, months, and even years of work. You deserve to be recognized for this special accomplishment.

But also, keep in mind that commencement is not only about you; it's about the people who helped support you to make it to this point. They want to see you in your cap and gown, walking across that stage, receiving your diploma. They want to cheer you on from the audience and take pictures of you and with you. They want to celebrate you and be proud of you on that special day.

Your degree will be with you the rest of your life, but this special occasion only comes once. Not going to commencement is like reading an entire book and then skipping the last chapter. It is something that everyone should do. If you do, you will likely be happy you did.

It is also highly recommended to buy a nice diploma frame to put your diploma in once you receive it—maybe a frame that has space for both your diploma and a picture of you in your cap and gown, alone or with those who helped you to make this dream a reality. Put this up on your wall in a prominent place for you and everyone else to see.

Not only does this diploma show customers and associates that you have the qualifications for your work, but it also shows pride in your degree. Putting this diploma up, even a picture with it, does one more thing that is very important: It is a constant reminder that all your hard work, your persistence and positive attitude, paid off. You accomplished your goal.

This is inspiration that you can be proud of for the rest of your life. It can also serve as a launching pad for other great successes in the future. Knowing that you can do this, and what it took to get here, you now have the confidence to anything you set your mind to.

To quote Rudyard Kipling,

> *"Yours is the Earth and everything that's in it."*

Nothing and no one can stop you now.

Conclusion

Anyone, regardless of age, skill level, or background, can be successful with online courses. It is about working hard AND working smart. No matter your learning style or individual needs, you can be successful.

Now that you have completed this book, it is time to put it into practice. Write out what you believe will work best for you and then start today. Keep in mind that learning is a process. You are never, ever at the finish line. This book gives you insight into the online world and will help you to be a success in this world.

Always remember that you will continually build upon this information and adapt it to your needs and style of learning. Use this book not only as a guide to getting started, or getting better, with your online experience but also as a launching pad for your life. The more you learn, the more you adapt to your specific situation, the stronger you will get. A little bit of discovery, *let's see if this works for me*, is what's needed. If it works, keep it—if it doesn't work as well as you expected, adapt and change it to make it work better for you.

Remember, you can be successful with online learning. Online has tremendous advantages and endless possibilities. Technology is forever growing and improving, making the online experience better every day. This mirrors the world that we live in today, tomorrow, and into the future.

Learn from the past, live in the present, and embrace the future. With your hard work today, there can be endless possibilities for what lies ahead. The only thing that can hold you back is you.

www.ingramcontent.com/pod-product-compliance
Lightning Source LLC
Chambersburg PA
CBHW041627220426
43663CB00004B/94